How Toys Work

Springs

Siân Smith

www.raintreepublishers.co.uk
Visit our website to find out more information about Raintree books.

To order:
☎ Phone 0845 6044371
📄 Fax +44 (0) 1865 312263
✉ Email myorders@raintreepublishers.co.uk

Customers from outside the UK please telephone +44 1865 312262

Raintree is an imprint of Capstone Global Library Limited, a company incorporated in England and Wales having its registered office at 7 Pilgrim Street, London, EC4V 6LB – Registered company number: 6695582

Edited by Dan Nunn, Rebecca Rissman, and Sian Smith
Designed by Joanna Hinton-Malivoire
Picture research by Mica Brancic
Production by Victoria Fitzgerald
Originated by Capstone Global Library Ltd
Printed and bound in China by South China Printing Company Ltd

ISBN 978 1 4062 3802 0
16 15 14 13 12
10 9 8 7 6 5 4 3 2 1

British Library Cataloguing in Publication Data
Smith, Sian.
  Springs. -- (How toys work)
  1. Springs (Mechanism)--Juvenile literature.
  I. Title II. Series
  621.8'24-dc22

Acknowledgements
The author and publisher are grateful to the following for permission to reproduce copyright material: Alamy p.15 (© Paul Weller); © Capstone Global Library Ltd pp.10, 11, 13, 16, 19 (Tudor Photography), 18, 20, 21 (Lord and Leverett); © Capstone Publishers pp.6, 9, 12, 17, 22c, 23 bottom, 7 main (Karon Dubke); istockphoto p.14 (© Ken Kan); Shutterstock pp.4 (© anki21), 4 (© BestPhotoPlus), 4 (© Nikolai Tsvetkov), 4 (© originalpunkt), 5 (© Losevsky Pavel), 8 (© Julián Rovagnati), 22a (© Andy Z.), 22b (© Ales Liska), 22d (© pio3), 23 top, 7 inset (© HomeStudio).

Cover photograph of slinky toys reproduced with permission of Alamy (© Yiap Views). Back cover photograph of wind-up toys reproduced with permission of © Capstone Global Library Ltd (Lord and Leverett).

We would like to thank David Harrison, Nancy Harris, Dee Reid, and Diana Bentley for their assistance in the preparation of this book.

Every effort has been made to contact copyright holders of material reproduced in this book. Any omissions will be rectified in subsequent printings if notice is given to the publisher.

Community Learning & Libraries
Cymuned Ddysgu a Llyfrgelloedd

This item should be returned or renewed by the last date stamped below.

Newport
CITY COUNCIL
CYNGOR DINAS
Casnewydd

Malpas Library & Information Centre

ENRICHING
LEARNING IN
NEWPORT
SCHOOLS

ELIN	
Z780823	
PETERS	05-Nov-2012
621.824	£10.99

Contents

Different toys

There are many different kinds
of toys.

Toys work in different ways.

Springs

Some toys use springs to work.

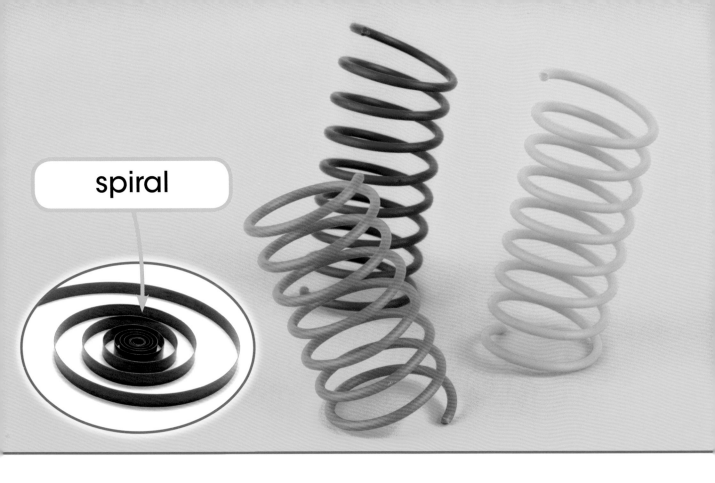

spiral

A spring is shaped like a spiral.

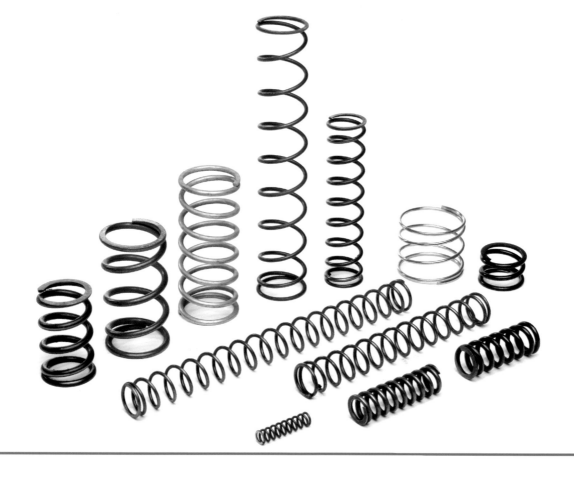

Springs can be made of metal.

spring

A jack-in-the-box uses a spring
to work.

Pushes and pulls

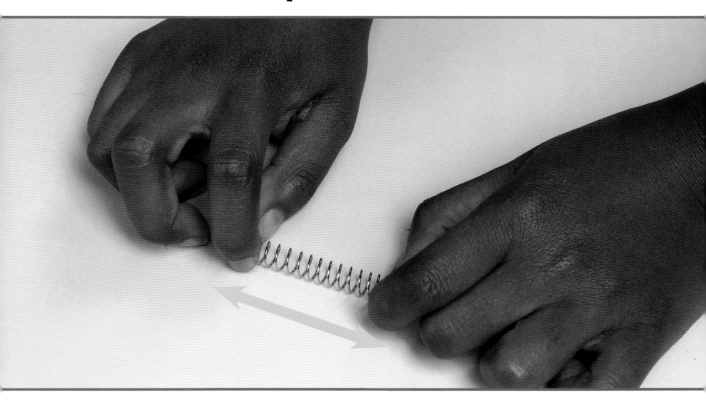

You can stretch a spring by pulling on it.

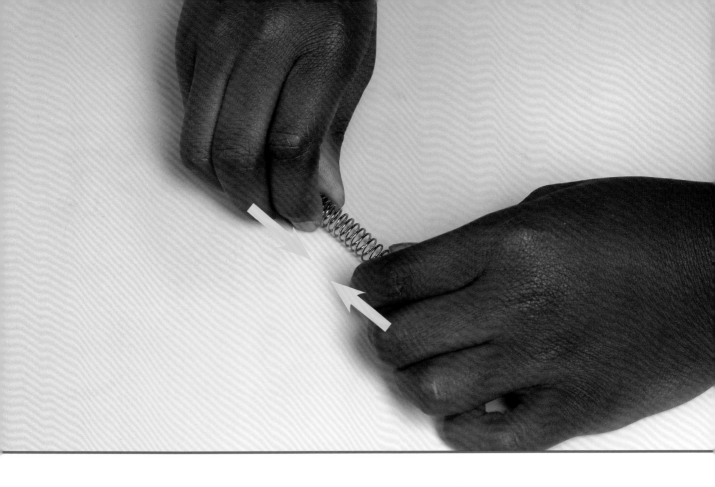

You can squash a spring by pushing it.

The spring pushes or pulls back again.
It tries to go back to its normal shape.

These pushes and pulls can make
toys move.

More toys with springs

Some toys bounce on springs.

This toy bounces on a spring.

spring

Some springs make balls move.

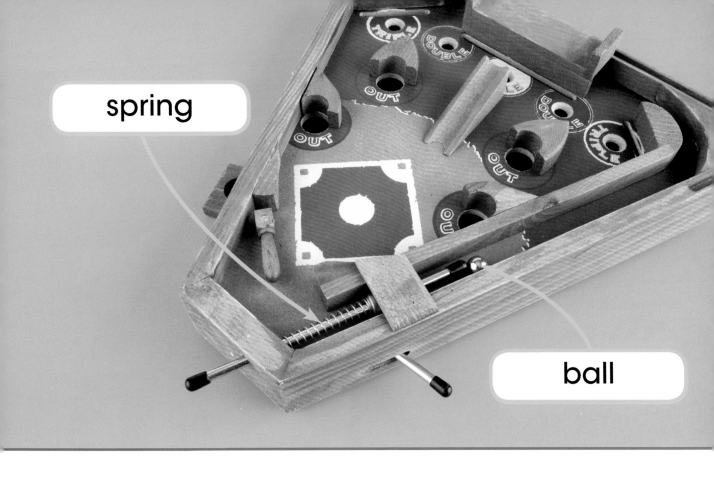

spring

ball

This spring makes a ball move.

Wind-up toys

Wind-up toys have springs inside.

When you wind up the toy, you squash the spring.

spring

The spring pushes out as it goes
back to its normal shape.

This makes the toy move along.

Quiz

Which one of these toys uses a spring to work?

Answer on page 24

Picture glossary

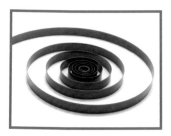

spiral a shape like a curl that winds round and round

spring most springs are made of metal. A spring is shaped like a spiral.

Index

Answer to question on page 22: Toy c uses a spring to work.

Notes for parents and teachers

Introduction

Show the children a collection of toys. One or more of the toys should work using a spring. Ask the children if they can spot the toy or toys with springs. Can they think of any other toys which use springs? Do they know what springs can do?

More information about springs

Explain that most springs are made out of metal because this makes them very strong, but springs can be made out of other materials too, such as plastic. Most springs are helix shaped, but for younger children it is easier to describe them as shaped like a spiral which curls round and round. They can create their own spring shape by wrapping a strip of paper around a pencil. When we push or pull a spring, we change its shape. The spring pushes or pulls back as it returns to its original shape. We use these pushes and pulls from springs to make things move.

Follow up activities

If possible take apart a simple clockwork toy so that the children can see the spring inside. They could go on to invent and draw their own toy which uses a spring or springs. For more advanced work on simple machines, children can work with an adult to discuss and play the games at: www.edheads.org/activities/simple-machines